The Bug Scientists

Damsel fly

by DONNA M. JACKSON

Houghton Mifflin Company Boston

Sources: Page 30, quotations from Valerie Cervenka's article in the
University of Minnesota Bell Museum of Natural History newsletter,
vol. 15, no. 1, spring 1998, are reprinted with the kind permission of
the author and the museum.
Page 44, excerpts from the Web page Encyclopedia Smithsonian:
Incredible Insects are reprinted with the kind permission of the
Smithsonian Institution.

www.houghtonmifflinbooks.com

The text of this book is set in Weiss and Bell Gothic.

Library of Congress Cataloging-in-Publication Data

Jackson, Donna M., 1959–
The bug scientist / by Donna M. Jackson.
p. cm.
Summary: Bug scientists, called entomologists, present information on
insects and explain how they use that information in their work.
RFN ISBN 0-618-10868-8 PAP ISBN 0-618-43232-9
1. Insects—Juvenile literature. 2. Entomologists—Juvenile literature.
[1. Insects. 2. Entomologists.] I. Title.

QL467.2 .K34 2002
595.7—dc21   2001039256

Printed in Singapore
TWP 10 9 8 7 6 5 4 3 2

Photo credits:

Max Badgley: p. 27 (left)

Liz Banfield Photography: pp. 22, 27 (right), 28, 30, 31

Scott Camazine, University of Pennsylvania: pp. 4, 14 (left), 15

Tom Campbell, Purdue University Agricultural Communications: pp. 7 (bottom), 9 (top)

Harry Chamberlain: p. 33

Chip Clark, Smithsonian Institution: p. 12

Clemson University Department of Entomology, Cooperative Extension Service: pp. 3, 5, 17 (top left), 44, 47

Helen Grooms: p. 26

Donna M. Jackson: pp. 7 (top), 8

Jim Kalisch and Leon Higley, Department of Entomology, University of Nebraska, Lincoln: pp. 10 (bottom), 14 (right), 25

Dave Knox: p. 45 (right)

Dr. Boris Kondratieff: p. 24

Janis Lentz: p. 20 (bottom)

Jim Lovett, Monarch Watch: pp. 20 (top), 21

Minneapolis Star Tribune: p. 31

Dr. Ted Schultz: pp. 35, 38

David Silk, *Minneapolis Star Tribune*: p. 29

Smithsonian Institution Office of Imaging, Printing and Photographic Services: p. 34

Paul B. Southerland: p. 19

Dave Umberger, Purdue University: pp. 6, 9 (bottom)

University of Florida, Department of Entomology and Nematology: pp. 17 (top right), 23, 45 (left)

Duncan Waddell, Nanoworld Image Gallery, University of Queensland, Australia: p. 13 (bottom)

Jim Wetterer, Associate Professor, Honors College, Florida Atlantic University: pp. 1, 10 (top), 11, 13 (top), 16, 17 (bottom left and right), 36, 37, 39, 40, 41, 42

To a wonderful family of bug-lovers:
Dan, Shelley, and the boys who keep them buzzing—Nathan, Losha, and Tioma

Camel cricket

Acknowledgments

A hercules beetle–sized thank you to all the bug scientists and others who took the time to share their work: Tom Turpin, Valerie Cervenka, Ted Schultz and the Smithsonian Institution, Steven Kutcher, Orley R. "Chip" Taylor and the Monarch Watch organization, Janis Lentz, Jade Then, Megan Prescott, Laurie Sides, Dr. Susan Roe, Liz Banfield, Ed Koday, Dave Umberger, Scott Camazine, James Kalisch, Olivia Maddox, Tom Campbell, Clyde Gorsuch, Dave Silk, John Capinera, James Castner, John L. Foltz, Dave Knox, Boris Kondratieff, Helen Grooms, Christine Turpin, Paul B. Southerland, Jim Lovett, Chip Clark, Duncan Waddell, Max Badgley and The Minneapolis Police Department.

I'm especially grateful to James Wetterer for generously sharing so many of his wonderful insect images, to Ann Rider for her keen editorial guidance, and to my honey bees, Charlie and Chris Jackson, who make it all worthwhile.

Weaver ants

**If an alien creature arrived on the planet Earth and
asked what the dominant life form was here,
we would have to say insects. To us, insects seem like
alien creatures, but in fact we're the aliens.**

—Ted Schultz, entomologist,
National Museum of Natural History, Smithsonian Institution

CONTENTS

Harlequin beetle

Professor
Tom Turpin

INSECT AMBASSADOR

The young contestant leans his head back, draws in a breath, and wraps his tongue around a slippery dead cricket. Seconds later he shoots the insect out of his mouth, and it lands 20 feet 2 1/2 inches away.

Some of the crowd wrinkle their faces in disgust, but all applaud enthusiastically. This "spit" is good for fourth place in Purdue University's annual Cricket Spitting Contest, one of many events featured at the school's annual Bug Bowl. Created in 1990 by Professor Tom Turpin and some of his colleagues, the Bug Bowl honors nature's least celebrated but most successful creatures on earth—insects.

How does spitting dead crickets *celebrate* insects?

"It's really a fun way to attract attention and get people to participate in the overall program," says Professor Turpin, who as ringmaster of the Bug Bowl is dressed in a top hat and tails decorated with dragonflies, ladybugs, and other assorted insects.

"Let's face it, many people dislike insects and might not stop by if we just offered the opportunity to see

A Bug's Best Friend

Professor Turpin grew up on a farm in Kansas, where he hit baseballs, collected insects, and kept honey bees. However, it wasn't until his college years that he decided to work with bugs for a living. That's when a professor showed him how he could combine his interest in biology (the study of all living organisms) and his love of agriculture by working with insects. Once bitten by the bug, he went on to earn a doctorate degree in entomology—the study of insects.

Some entomologists, or bug scientists, work at museums or zoos, where they collect insects, identify new species, and investigate the relationships between bugs and the rest of the natural world. Others work for the federal government or with companies that specialize in controlling insects that are considered pests, such as those that harm crops or cause diseases.

Professor Turpin shares his appreciation for insects by teaching college students, a few of whom may decide to become entomologists themselves. And, as he does with the Bug Bowl, he teaches with a theatrical twist. To

insects under a microscope," he says. "Having a cricket-spitting contest attracts the attention of newspapers and television reporters, who spread the news about the event. Once people come to see the contest, we hope they'll also wander over to the insect petting zoo and the honey bee demonstration to learn more about these fascinating creatures."

illustrate lessons, Professor Turpin turns his classrooms into a mini Broadway for bugs.

One day he slips on a chef's hat and entices students to eat trail mix called "Caterpillar Crunch" and fried mealworms, which are commonly eaten in some cultures. Another day he arrives in class with a pith helmet and a butterfly net to demonstrate the life of a bug collector.

The technique works. Professor Turpin has received many teaching awards, including Professor of the Year for Indiana. His classes are among Purdue University's most popular, with more than 450 students enrolling in his introductory insect science course each semester.

"People learn more when they're having fun," he says. "I like to get them to think about and do things they hadn't thought about before." That includes racing cockroaches, eating "Chocolate Chirpy Chip Cookies" (made with dry-roasted crickets), and reading about insects in poems, stories, and songs, such as this Chippewa children's chant:

Opposite: **Creating insect art at the Bug Bowl**
Right: **Professor Turpin as "beekeeper"**
Below: **Outdoor classroom**

The Firefly

Flitting white-fire insect,
waving white-fire bug,
give me light before I go to sleep!
Come, little dancing white-fire bug,
come, little flitting white-fire beast,
light me with your bright white flame,
your little candle!

Taking the "ug" out of Bug

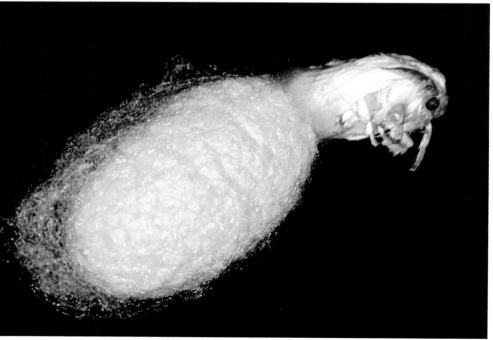

"Insects have been given a bad rap," says Professor Turpin. Many people see them only as bothersome pests who bite, sting, carry diseases, and damage trees and plants. But fewer than 5 percent of insects are pests, he says. "Insects bring far more benefits to the earth than harm."

One benefit is providing people with valuable goods and services. Bees, for instance, give us honey and beeswax, which is used to make candles and is a key ingredient in many lotions and lipsticks. The cocoons of the silkworm supply us with silk, a lustrous fiber used to make clothing.

Insects pollinate (fertilize with pollen) the plants that give us many of our fruits, vegetables, and nuts. Some control undesirable pests that harm crops. Others help keep the earth clean by eating dead animals. (Otherwise the roads would be littered with carcasses!) And the billions of tiny insects that live in the dirt keep the soil aerated and alive, explains Professor Turpin.

Insects are also important in the laboratory. "Scientists use fruit flies in genetic research and teaching

Dung beetles roll animal droppings into a ball, bury it in the soil, and lay their eggs on it. When the young hatch, they have a ready supply of food.

because they're easy to grow, they reproduce rapidly, and they have big chromosomes," says Professor Turpin. An international research team recently mapped the entire DNA (deoxyribonucleic acid) coding of the fruit fly. DNA is the chemical blueprint that makes us who we are and is important because about two thirds of the genes known to cause illnesses in people—including cancer and Parkinson's disease—are also found in this particular fruit fly. By figuring out the tiny creature's genetic coding, researchers hope to learn more about human genetic diseases.

Butterflies, bumble bees, and other insects appeal to our aesthetic sense. Their fluttering wings and fascinating colors and shapes serve as inspiration for everything from paintings and postage stamps to dresses and jewelry. In China and Japan people listen to the soothing sounds of live crickets and other singing insects, a pastime that has been enjoyed for centuries.

Some insects have become objects of worship. The ancient Greek cult of Artemis revered the bee, and the Egyptians chose the scarab, or dung beetle, as a symbol

of their sun god, Ra. Ra rolled the sun across the sky and buried it at night, much the way the scarab beetle rolls a ball of dung, or animal droppings, into its nest when it's ready to lay eggs.

With all these important links to our lives, it's easy to understand why Professor Turpin believes bugs deserve a break and why he's become an insect ambassador. Along with teaching university courses, Professor Turpin writes books and newspaper columns about insects, talks about them on national television shows, travels the country

Abdomen   **Thorax**   **Head**

Grasshopper

making school presentations, and sings the praises of bugs on public radio.

Small is beautiful, he contends. Compared with other animals, insects can run faster and jump higher, making them nature's gold-medal Olympians. "Some grasshoppers have been observed to jump nearly ten times their height and twenty times their length," says Professor Turpin. "If humans could do that, just think what the world records for the high jump and the long jump might be!"

The small size of insects also allows them to uphold their status as the most successful creatures on the planet. Not only are they earth's best fliers and farmers, they've been living here for about 350 million years. Humans have been on the planet for only 10,000 years.

"Insects make up about 80 percent of all known animals," explains Professor Turpin. They live on land, in water, on plants, and even inside other animals' bodies. "More than 1 million species of insects have been described, and many more—some say as many as 10 to 30 million—have yet to be named."

Bug Basics

Many people think that spiders, centipedes, and all other tiny creatures are insects. But that is not the case. Adult insects have six legs, one or two pairs of wings, and two antennae. An insect's body is covered by an exoskeleton (a hard outer shell) and is divided into three distinct parts: head, thorax, and abdomen. A spider, in contrast, has two main body parts—head and abdomen—and belongs to a related class of animals called arachnids. "An insect's head has a pair of compound eyes—compound because they have more than one lens—which gives them a mosaic-like view of the world; two antennae to feel and smell; and a mouth," says Professor Turpin.

Insects' mouthparts come in different forms, depending on what they eat. The housefly's mouth soaks up liquid food like a sponge. The assassin bug has a powerful rostrum or beak that pierces and sucks out the insides of other bugs.* Butterflies and moths have a hoselike tube (called a proboscis) for sipping nectar from flowers, and grasshoppers' mouths can rip off and "chew" pieces of plants.

Above: **Spiders are not insects, because they have two main body parts instead of three.**

Below: **The compound eyes of the housefly contain hundreds of tiny lenses shaped like stop signs.**

*While most people use the words *bug* and *insect* to mean the same thing, scientists consider only insects that have mouthparts that pierce and suck as true bugs.

Left: **A praying mantis uses its legs for grasping its food.**

Opposite: **Can you find the walking stick?**

An insect's middle region, or thorax, is made for movement. It carries three pairs of legs and one or two pairs of wings. "Like the mouthparts, the legs differ among insects," explains Professor Turpin. Cockroaches use their legs for running; crickets use them for jumping; water bugs, for swimming; and praying mantises, for grasping.

An insect's abdomen, the rear segment, allows it to breathe, excrete wastes, and reproduce. An insect breathes through a series of holes, called spiracles, that are found along both sides of its abdomen. The spiracles connect to breathing tubes called tracheae, which help carry oxygen throughout the insect's body.

Left: **A firefly's light produces no heat. It's the result of a chemical reaction that takes place in its abdomen.**

Masters of Survival

With just three segments to work with—head, thorax, and abdomen—nature has fashioned insects into some of the most intricate and exquisite living sculptures imaginable, all to help them survive and adapt to their environment.

"Insects are extremely creative," says Professor Turpin, who finds their ability to adapt one of their most fascinating qualities. "Almost any survival technique that exists on the earth you'll find in insects."

Many insects use camouflage to blend in with their surroundings and hide from predators. Walking sticks, for example, can make themselves look like twigs, and the wings of some tropical katydids look like healthy green leaves. Cunning caterpillars even masquerade as bird droppings.

To scare off their enemies, some "copycat" insects mimic the shape, sound, or appearance of a dangerous animal, such as a snake. Others disguise themselves as an insect that stings, tastes bad, or contains poison. The drone fly uses its black and yellow stripes to masquerade as a stinging bee, but in fact it's harmless.

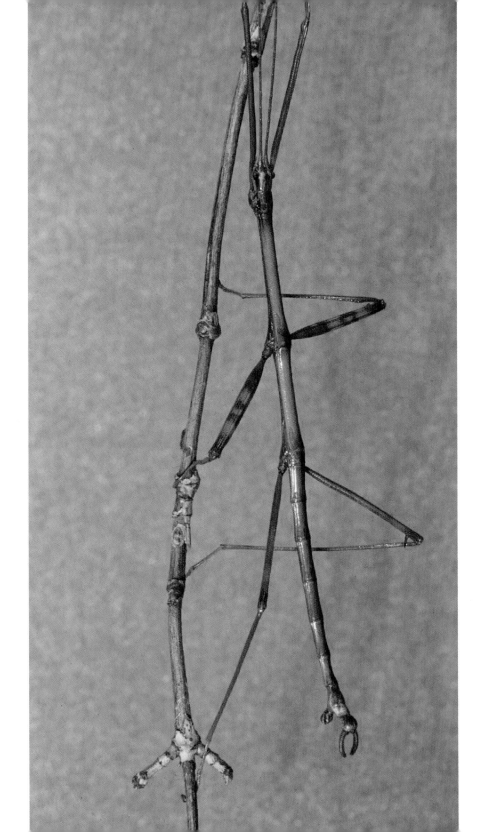

Bright colors on an insect also warn predators to stay away. The stinkbug's colorful design tells attackers, "I smell bad and will spray a stinky-smelling chemical in the air if you come too close to me!" And the bombardier beetle sprays predators with an amazing hot chemical mixture, so blistering it can reach the temperature of boiling water.

"I tell my students that insects survive in one of two ways," says Professor Turpin. "One is by the sheer force of numbers—ninety-nine are hatched so that one survives and reproduces. And the other is by being creative and avoiding becoming a meal for something else. There's a reason old Ferdie [his pet chicken] won't eat a red-colored insect . . . He knows they taste bad. But give him an old brown mealworm and he's a happy camper."

Left, top: **Predaceous stink bug attacking a green stink bug.** Above: **A ladybug munches on aphids. Its bright colors warn predators that it will squirt a bitter, yellow fluid if they come too close. Chemicals that make bugs taste bad often come from the plants they eat.** Left: **Tree hoppers resemble thorns on a rosebush.** Right: **A hawk moth caterpillar mimicks a snake.**

17

MONARCH BUTTERFLY WATCH

"I couldn't tell one butterfly from another," says Jade Then, a fifth-grade student at C. C. Mason Elementary in Cedar Park, Texas. Now she's practically a monarch butterfly expert. Jade has reared monarch caterpillars, fed them milkweed, and anxiously watched as they've transformed into butterflies — thanks in part to her teacher, Janis Lentz, and an international program called Monarch Watch.

Monarch Watch is a network of students, teachers, volunteers, and researchers who are dedicated to studying monarch butterflies and promoting their conservation.

No other butterflies in the world migrate like the monarchs of North America, says Dr. Orley R. "Chip" Taylor, director of the program based at the University of Kansas. "Monarchs travel up to three thousand miles and are the only butterflies to make such a long, two-way migration every year," he says. "Amazingly, they fly south in masses to the same winter roosts (resting spots) in Mexico and California — often to the same trees!"

Learning more about the monarch butterflies' migration is a primary goal of Monarch Watch. In fact, one of its key projects involves distributing identification tags to students and others to place on butterflies so that researchers can collect migration information.

Jade and her classmates tagged eighty-six butterflies last fall. "We looked up in the sky and chased the butterflies with

Tagged monarch

The label on the butterfly's wing reads:

UNIV. KS
MAIL
ENTOMOLOGY
LAWRENCE
KS 66045
PZ 512
:01

nets on the playground," she explains. Before tagging the butterflies, Jade noted whether the butterfly was male or female: males have thin vein pigmentation and swollen pouches on their hindwings, and females have thick vein pigmentation and no pouches on their hindwings. She also noted the air temperature, the wind speed, and whether the butterfly was in good condition. Then, "one person held the butterfly down," she says, "while the other tagged it in the mitten-shaped area [called the discal cell] under the wing."

When people find the tagged monarchs and report them back to the program, it allows researchers to estimate the size of the monarch population and figure out how many butterflies made it to their destination. (Current figures are from 20 to 45 percent.) It also helps answer questions such as *How does the weather influence migration?* and *Do migrations differ from year to year?*

"The biggest mystery is the navigation and how they know where to go," says Dr. Taylor. "Studies point to some kind of magnetic orientation using the earth's magnetic field, but the critical data needed to support this isn't available yet." The

Monarchs blanket their winter homes in clusters.

issue is complicated further because butterflies use other ways to navigate, he says. "For example, we know that they also use the sky, the position of the sun, and the time of day."

While Dr. Taylor investigates the mysteries of the monarchs, Janis Lentz and her students check e-mail daily for butterfly updates from Monarch Watch. In the fall, they read reports about the mass of butterflies that head south through Texas to the Oyamel Forests of Central Mexico. Here millions of monarchs cluster in the oyamel fir trees to keep warm and dry during the winter months.

"Around February 14, the monarchs come out and start searching for a mate before taking the journey back north," explains Lentz. "This generation goes to Texas and lays eggs, and then their offspring head further north."

In September, the great- (great-) grandchildren of the monarchs who originally spent the winter in Mexico will find themselves spread across the United States and Canada when they will suddenly decide it's time to fill themselves with nectar and start the journey south. And so the cycle will begin again.

Valerie Cervenka

CRIME-FIGHTING INSECT INVESTIGATOR

"The Bug Lady" teams with police to solve crimes.

Blow flies arrive first when a dead body is left outdoors.

WARNING: this section may be hazardous to your lunch.

That's how Valerie Cervenka, Minnesota's only forensic entomologist, begins most of her slide shows, even the ones she presents to the police. While many officers have encountered grisly crime scenes, most still squirm in their seats when they see maggots (fly larvae) snacking on dead bodies.

"It may seem gruesome, but the [insects] are actually performing a necessary role in the life and death cycle," explains Cervenka, whom many people call "the Bug Lady." "Insects are decomposers—natural recyclers of decaying animal flesh. Without their help, we could be thigh-high in roadkill and other dead animals."

We might also have a few more unsolved crimes. That's because doing what comes naturally to insects enables them to perform another important but little-known service: crime fighting.

Murder, She Buzzed

Imagine walking in the woods and stumbling upon a dead body. Now imagine seeing hundreds of maggots feeding on that body while a few large beetles dart about. Not a pretty picture, but one that Cervenka witnesses when investigators call on her to help crack complex cases in which insects are found at the scene.

How do bugs help solve crimes? Primarily by leading predictable lives.

The life cycle of the blow fly moves from egg (left) to larva (maggots, right) to pupa (cocoon, top) to adult fly.

Within hours after a body has been abandoned outdoors, waves of insects swarm to the scene. The first to arrive are usually blow flies, who are attracted to odors of decomposition that human noses can't detect. The blow flies feed, mate, and lay eggs, which pass through distinct stages of growth: from egg to larva (the maggot stage) to pupa (the cocoon stage) and finally to the adult stage.

By examining these insects and tracing back to the time when their eggs were laid, Cervenka can help officials arrive at an approximate time of death. Knowing the time of death helps investigators reconstruct events and narrow the list of suspects if they think a crime has been committed.

The Testimony of Bugs

Bugs have been fighting crimes for centuries, says Cervenka. "The first record of using insects to solve a crime dates back to a Chinese manual of forensic medicine

Right: **Pig carcass
infested with blow flies**
Below: **Blow fly maggots**

written in 1235 A.D. by Sung Tz'u," she explains. The book, *Washing Away of Wrongs*, describes the mysterious murder of a Chinese villager slashed with a rice sickle. When routine attempts to track the killer failed, investigators set up an ingenious trap. Knowing that flies would be attracted to the scent of blood, they called local farmers to line up outside, placing their sickles in front of them. Almost immediately, flies swarmed to one of the blades—exposing the murderer, who broke down and confessed.

In 1850, a case in France marked the first known use of insect evidence in the Western world, says Cervenka. When a plasterer discovered a body behind a mantelpiece he was repairing, detectives called Dr. Bergeret d'Arbois to investigate. After examining the insects and mites on the remains, Dr. d'Arbois concluded that the body had been concealed since 1848, before the current owners had moved in. "By using insect evidence, he was able to eliminate the homeowners as suspects," says Cervenka.

The Bug Lady

Nature has always fascinated Valerie Cervenka. Growing up in Minnesota, she watched birds and gathered wildflowers with her mother and her great-aunt Nora, an artist who painted the world around her. Young Valerie collected grasshoppers in jars and snakes in shoeboxes. She befriended a Canada goose, turtles, and some stray salamanders.

"Val found the salamanders in the window wells of our basement," remembers her mother, Helen Grooms. Soon she adopted the lizardlike amphibians as pets. "She moved them into the garage and fed them earthworms."

Cervenka's early love of plants and animals resurfaced in college at the University of Minnesota. But it was her first entomology class with an enthusiastic professor that changed the direction of her life.

"I was hooked," she says. "I started looking at insects under a microscope and discovered how beautiful and fascinating they are." She found herself reading laboratory manuals at the breakfast table, collecting insects, and memorizing their scientific names. "I loved knowing the names of insects and being able to talk about their life histories," she says.

Cervenka went on to earn a bachelor's and a master's degree in entomology, as well as a bachelor's degree in horticulture, the study of plants under cultivation. After college she worked in California researching ways to control grape leafhoppers with "beneficial" bugs instead of pesticides. Beneficial bugs feed or lay their eggs on insects considered to be harmful. When the eggs hatch, the offspring eat away at the bug they're living on and eventually kill it.

Below: **One of Val's first "bug" jobs was to help control grape leafhoppers, which can damage grape leaves.**

Right: **Collecting and identifying insects continues to fascinate Cervenka.**

Why is it important to control grape leafhoppers? "They not only damage grape leaves," explains Cervenka, "but they form such thick clouds at harvest time that workers have difficulty picking the grapes."

A few years later Cervenka returned to Minnesota to work as a livestock entomologist, studying natural ways to control stable flies, which suck blood from cattle and other livestock. "These flies prevent cattle from gaining weight by biting so relentlesssly that the cows spend more

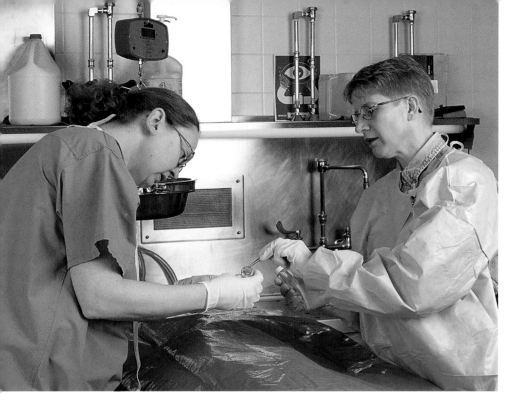

Val and Dr. Susan Roe meet in the morgue to collect insects on dead bodies.

closely with Dr. Susan Roe, an assistant medical examiner who immediately recognized the benefits of having an insect expert on her forensics team.

"I'll never forget the first time Val walked into the morgue," says Dr. Roe. "She said she didn't know if she could handle touching the dead bodies. I said, 'The *bodies?*' Frankly, the most disgusting part of my job is handling the maggots!"

Unraveling Mysteries with Maggots

Dr. Susan Roe performs autopsies for the Ramsey County Medical Examiner's Office in St. Paul. It's her job to determine the cause and manner of a person's death: Did he or she die naturally or by accident? Was a crime involved?

Most of the time the work is straightforward, and there's plenty of physical evidence to answer essential

time stomping and swishing than feeding," says Cervenka. "Calves also have a hard time nursing when mom is stomping all the time or heading to the pond for relief!"

During this time Cervenka attended an intriguing presentation about forensic entomology. The work so fascinated her that she added another job title to her resume: insect investigator.

"I figured my expertise was working with flies, and I didn't mind maggots," she says. "So after the symposium, I asked the speakers how I could break into the field."

The next month Cervenka offered her services to two local medical examiner's offices. She began working

**Size and timeline of
blow fly development**

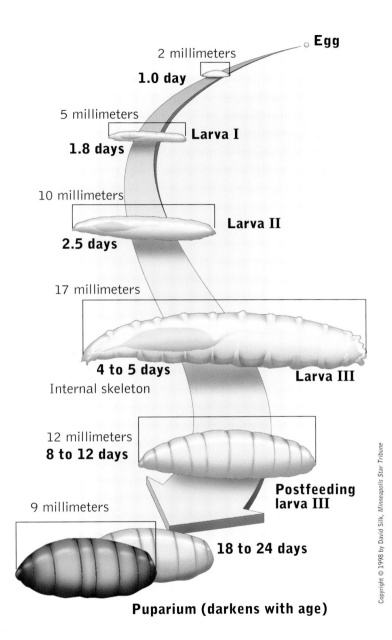

2 millimeters
1.0 day
o **Egg**

5 millimeters
1.8 days
Larva I

10 millimeters
2.5 days
Larva II

17 millimeters
4 to 5 days
Internal skeleton
Larva III

12 millimeters
8 to 12 days
**Postfeeding
larva III**

9 millimeters
18 to 24 days
Puparium (darkens with age)

questions such as when the person died. "Ninety percent of the bodies we get have been dead for a few days, maybe a week," says Dr. Roe. "And the sooner you see a person after death, the easier it is to tell the time of death."

But some bodies aren't discovered right away, and they begin to decompose. "Some people die a natural death but aren't found right away because they're in locked houses or apartments. Others are crime victims who have been purposely hidden, buried, or abandoned in isolated areas and found through happenstance."

These are the cases that require Cervenka's special forensic entomology skills.

"When I'm called in to work on a case, I try to visit the crime scene to collect specimens. This is preferable . . . because police officers are generally not trained in the collection and preservation of insect specimens," she says. Most times, however, her work is done in the medical examiner's office.

Cervenka begins by pulling out her bug-collecting kit, which contains items such as forceps, labels, an insect

eggs

1st instar larvae (maggots)

2nd instar

3rd instar

pupae

adults

Blow flies at various stages of development

net, and vials filled with ethyl alcohol to preserve specimens. Next she surveys the body, looking for evidence of blow flies and other insects. The presence of blow fly eggs or first-stage larvae (maggots 2 millimeters long) tells her that the body has been exposed for twenty-four hours or less; larger maggots (up to 17 millimeters long) suggest that the corpse has been decaying for a few days up to a few weeks, depending on the air temperature. Warmer temperatures speed up the development of insects, and colder temperatures slow it down.

When collecting specimens, Cervenka looks for the largest maggots "because these will be the oldest and provide the most accurate estimate of when flies could have

first laid eggs." She keeps some alive to rear to adulthood in her refrigerator at home and preserves the rest in alcohol. Cervenka also collects any other insects that might be present, such as beetles, because different insects arrive at different stages of decay. In addition, she notes where a body was found (for example, in a trunk, in the woods, or underwater), because location affects when the first blow flies arrive. "This helps me paint as clear a picture as possible of what was going on at the scene," she says.

After the specimens are collected, Cervenka gathers temperature data from the weather station nearest the death scene. "Once I determine how the temperature and other variables would have affected the flies' growth cycle, I can calculate how many days it has taken for the immature flies to develop into their present stage. By counting backward in this way, I arrive at the day when the flies probably began laying eggs on the body."

One time Cervenka was called in to check out a body found at a park. Initially she thought it had been there for years because "it looked like a mummy from the science

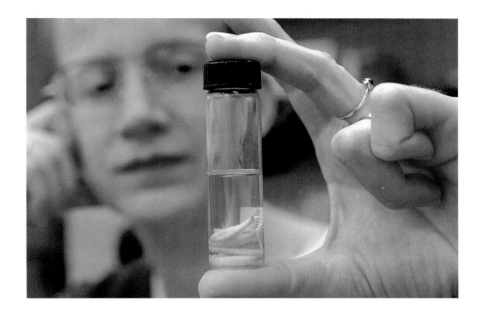

Val inspects a vial of maggots. Maggots help her identify time of death.

museum. The skin was black, leathery, and dry." After collecting the few pupae and dung beetles at the scene and researching weather data, she discovered that the body actually had been there for only about six weeks. "I was shocked," she says. Apparently, the summer sun had accelerated the decomposition process.

Time of death is not the only clue bugs can provide. In certain cases, they may help determine the cause of death. For example, if insects are found in parts of the body that usually do not attract bugs—like the shoulders or thighs— it often indicates that there have been injuries to those area. Insects such as blow flies are attracted to moist sites and tend to lay their eggs around wounds with blood. The types of insects found—or a lack of insects altogether—tell other tales.

When insects that are found only in the city turn up on a body found in a rural area, it indicates that the body has been moved. That's also the case when bugs native to one part of the country are discovered on a body found someplace else. The presence of some insects even reveals the season when a crime occurred and whether it happened during the day or at night. When no bugs are found on a body that's outdoors, which is extremely unusual in warm months, it may mean that the body has been frozen and recently left outside.

On some occasions, insects have revealed to forensic entomologists that the material they're working with isn't even human. In one case Cervenka was given a piece of something that looked like a human liver. After examining the maggots on it, she determined they were larvae of the crane fly, which feeds on decaying fungi. Turns out the "human liver" was really a piece of dried lobster mushroom!

bug bits

HOLLYWOOD BUG DIRECTOR
Lights. Camera. Action!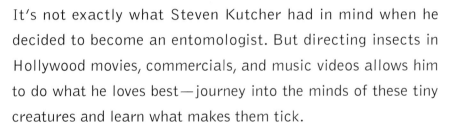

It's not exactly what Steven Kutcher had in mind when he decided to become an entomologist. But directing insects in Hollywood movies, commercials, and music videos allows him to do what he loves best—journey into the minds of these tiny creatures and learn what makes them tick.

"It's creative problem-solving," says Kutcher, whose movie work includes *Jurassic Park*, *Arachnophobia*, and *James and the Giant Peach*. "Not only do I have to figure out what the insect or spider can do, I have to take that behavior and adapt it to what the movie requires."

Take the time he persuaded an ant to walk to the end of a stick and "wave" to a movie camera. Actually, it didn't take a lot of coaxing. Being a bug expert, Kutcher knew that ants wiggle their antennae—their primary sense organs—to scope out their surroundings. Sure enough, when the ant reached the end of the stick, it wiggled its antennae. To viewers it looked like a friendly "hello."

The bug director's also convinced a cockroach to run across the floor, then flip over on its back and persuaded bees to swarm around a beekeeper for a fried chicken commercial.

Kutcher's fascination with insects began when he collected fireflies in the Catskill Mountains of New York as a child. "My family would go up there every summer," he says. "The Catskills have lakes, streams, and lots of rainfall, and I loved to play in the water and explore nature."

It wasn't long before the insect enthusiast brought his habit home and began collecting pill bugs, beetles, and butterflies from his parents' garden and keeping them in his bedroom. "There were so many bugs to find by turning over rocks and logs," he says. "I would try to figure out all the mysteries of

Steven Kutcher directs insects and spiders in movies and music videos.

nature by asking questions like *Who made this web?* and *What insect lives here?*"

When it came time to pick a profession, entomology seemed a natural fit. "It's a profession that combines science and art and allows you to go out into the field and study nature," he says. In graduate school Kutcher even added comedy to the mix when he worked at a radio station answering listeners' bug questions and playing bug songs, such as "Shoo Fly" and "Flight of the Bumble Bee."

Today, along with his Hollywood pursuits, Kutcher works to teach people about conservation and the importance of open space. "I've had the opportunity to travel all over," he says, "and I've observed how the places to collect insects have diminished, along with the native insects that live there."

That worries him because he wants children to have the same opportunity to interact with nature that he had when he was young and to perhaps find their passion and create a career. "I don't think I would be as passionate about nature if I didn't have the opportunity to explore open spaces when I was a child," he says.

Ted Schultz

THE OLD MACDONALD OF THE ANT WORLD

Dr. Schultz studies ant specimens—dead and preserved—under the microscope.

As a boy, Ted Schultz was fascinated by ants.

What amazed Ted Schultz about ants as a child still amazes him as an adult. "We grow up thinking that ants are the most lowly creatures on the planet, because their brains are minuscule," he says. "Nonetheless, they're social insects with a collective intelligence that's capable of complicated behaviors. And what's so fascinating is that these incredibly complex behaviors have striking parallels to human behaviors."

Honey ants, for example, "tend cattle" just the way humans do. The only difference is that their cattle are small insects called aphids. "The ants protect these 'cattle' from predators," explains Dr. Schultz. "They milk the aphids for the sweet honeydew that they produce and consume it as a nutritious reward. In some cases the ants herd the aphids from plant to plant."

Ants war with one another and practice slavery. "Some ant colonies raid other ant colonies, take the babies, and raise them as their slaves," says Dr. Schultz.

Ants also manipulate tools as humans do. Weaver ants use their babies, the larvae, as "sewing machines" to quilt together large leaves for their nests. While worker ants grab the edges of two leaves with their jaws and pull them together so that they meet, other ants hold the larvae in their jaws and walk back and forth between the leaf edges, sewing them together with strands of silk produced by the larvae.

Ants even have their own pets, says Dr. Schultz. "In an ant colony, there are other insects and arthropods that spend their entire lives living with the ants and begging them for food."

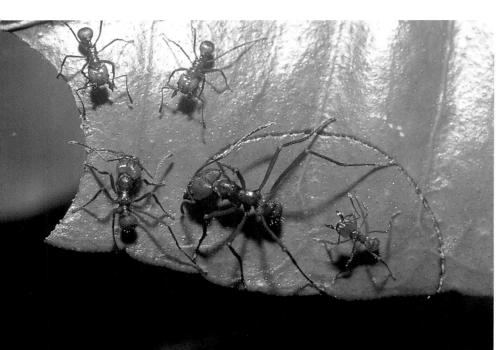

Left: **Most Attini ants live in South and Central America.** Below: **Attini ants on a grapefruit leaf**

These and other facts about the social behavior of ants intrigued Ted Schultz as a child when he read a book by G. Collins Wheat called *The World of Ants: How they Live, Work and Communicate Within Their Colonies*—a book that he still keeps a copy of today. What amazed him most, however, was finding out that some ants farmed their food instead of hunting it. "How could that be possible?" he thought.

Today, Dr. Schultz is a research entomologist at the Smithsonian Institution in Washington, D.C., and is one of only a handful of myrmecologists (scientists who study ants) who make their livings studying Attini ants, which are farmer ants.

Attini ants don't grow corn or wheat in fields, as humans have been doing for about ten thousand years. Instead they tend fungus gardens. More than two hundred known species of Attini ants—including the well-known leaf-cutter ants—plant white, fuzzy fungi, which they fertilize and weed so it will thrive. It's an agricultural lifestyle they have perfected over 50 million years, and it's one Dr. Schultz believes humans can ultimately learn from.

Left: **Leaf-cutting ants can carry up to thirty times their own weight.** Right: **Large worker ants cut leaves, while small workers guard them against attack.**

Ants with Plants

Scientists have known about farmer ants since the late 1800s, but until recently little was known about the mutually beneficial relationship (or symbiosis) between the ants and the fungi. This surprised Dr. Schultz, who, as a graduate student at Cornell University, decided he would devote his life's work to figuring out the origin of the ants' fungus-growing behavior and the way it evolved over time.

Most Attini ants live in South and Central America, but about a dozen species live in the southern United States and as far north as New Jersey and southern Illinois. Dr. Schultz's first glimpse of Attini ants came in 1991, when he traveled to Costa Rica with twenty other students for a tropical-studies field course.

"A lot of different species were there," he says. "In fact, farmer ants are so successful in the tropics that if you had x-ray vision and could look underground across a whole patch of jungle, you'd see a fungus garden about every square foot."

Dr. Schultz digs for ants in Brazil.

The most conspicuous farmer ants in Costa Rica are the leaf-cutters, he says. "Their ant mounds can literally be a twenty-foot by twenty-foot churned-up area of the ground with thousands of chambers under the surface. Their colonies can contain millions of ants that together might weigh as much as an adult cow." While watching the leaf-cutters, Dr. Schultz observed many ants running on little roads. "There were ants with nothing in their mandibles [jaws] running out of the nest and ants with leaf pieces up to thirty times their weight running in."

It's easy to think that the leaf pieces are food for the ants, but they're not. The ants chew the leaves into a mulchlike substance and add it to their fungus gardens. They then transfer healthy, growing fungus from elsewhere in the garden to the mulch. Finally, they apply ant droppings to the growing gardens. The droppings contain enzymes (substances that produce a chemical reaction), which help the garden fungus digest the mulch. As the fungus grows, it produces structures called gongylidia (gong-ee-lid-ee-ah), which serve as a nutri-

tious food for the ants in the colony. This food is easy for the ants to harvest.

While the ants that cut leaves are easy to spot, the more primitive Attini ants that grow fungus gardens are very hard to find, explains Dr. Schultz. "When you do find them, you see one ant at a time, walking very slowly, carrying bits of fungus food and going into a little nondescript hole in the ground. If you disturb one of those ants, it curls up and plays dead, unlike the leaf-cutter ants, who freak out and send their giant soldiers with big heads to come and bite you!"

Once Dr. Schultz finds the entrance to a nest, he takes out his trowel and digs down about one to three feet below the surface until he sees a chamber that contains a fungus garden.

"The fungus looks like a very thick, white cottony fuzz that can range from about the size of a walnut to that of a softball," he says. "It's a spongelike mass, laced with passageways and tunnels, that grows on top of all the food the ants have brought in." Depending on the species of

ant, that food can be anything from seeds to little bits of flowers that have fallen in the forest.

As on human farms, weeds often invade ant gardens. To prevent them from destroying the crop, the ants wiggle their way through the tunnels of fungus and pluck out any harmful molds and bacteria they find. Once they dispose of the weeds, they clean themselves to keep from reintroducing the "weeds" to the garden.

Attini ants also use antibiotics, a substance that destroys or prevents the growth of microorganisms, explains Dr. Schultz. "There's a particular weed fungus that specializes in infecting their fungus gardens. The weed sneaks in and lies low until something goes slightly wrong with the garden, then it takes its opportunity to attack." To control this parasite, Attini ants grow cultures on their bodies of a special kind of bacteria that works only against this weed.

Diversity Makes the Difference

A new Attini ant garden begins when the ant queen takes a bite from the fungus garden, stores it in a pouch in her mouth, and flies off to mate. Once she has mated, she digs a new nest, plants the tiny starter fungus, and begins laying hundreds of eggs. The queen then tends both the garden and the eggs until the offspring mature and take over the farm duties.

Because an ant queen starts a new nest using fungus from an old garden, scientists used to think that all the nests of a particular ant species descended from the same original fungus. However, Dr. Schultz and his colleagues analyzed the DNA of more than five hundred fungus samples taken from the most primitive Attini ants and found some surprising news: different nests of the same ant species often grow different fungi.

"Ants appear to be going out and bringing back a brand-new fungus for their gardens on occasion," says Dr. Schultz. Apparently they also borrow or steal fungus from their neighbors when necessary, because various ant species grow the same fungus.

Opposite: **Attini ant queen on her fungus garden. Queens can live more than fifteen years.**

Below: **Ants on an orange**
Right: **Attini queen and worker ant on a fungus garden**

Growing many kinds of fungus is an important long-term, evolutionary strategy, says Dr. Schultz. "Most ant farmers cultivate a diversity of crops rather than committing exclusively to a single one." This keeps the ants from starving to death and being wiped out if a disease spreads through one of their crops.

Some Attini ants collect fallen buds instead of leaf-cuttings.

"We're just coming to better understand one of the great wonders of nature," says Dr. Schultz. "Biologists are becoming more aware of the role of symbiosis in evolution. It's an important way organisms evolve, and the ant-fungus relationship is a good example. The ants feed the fungus, keep away its competitors, carry it through generations, and distribute it." The fungus, in turn, provides food for the ants and allows them to thrive.

In addition, "Attini ants have been growing the same crop for 50 million years, so humans can probably learn about sustainable agriculture from them."

Dr. Schultz says we also can learn about antibiotics from the ants—especially since ants have successfully fought off strains of bacteria for millions of years.

Insect Frontiers

When Dr. Schultz is not traveling to tropical locations collecting live ants to study, he researches dead ants at the Smithsonian. "We have a vast collection here that's a giant reference library of ants from around the world," he explains. By studying dead specimens, Dr. Schultz learns more about ant anatomy and is able to determine how the species are related to one another. He also spends time conducting DNA studies on ants in a molecular lab, collaborating with other scientists on projects, and reading and writing about ants to better understand their evolutionary family tree.

To gain insights into ant behavior, Dr. Schultz tends about twenty-five colonies of fungus-growing ants in small plastic boxes next door to his office. "This allows me to see all the life stages of the larvae as well as all the males, females, and queens—something I can't do out in the field."

Working with insects is great fun, with many opportunities for discovery, says Dr. Schultz. "There's a vast frontier out there, of which we know very little. Of the one million insect species we've identified, all we know about most is the name that we've given them." With an estimated 10 to 30 million more insects still to be discovered, that leaves a lot of work to be done!

AMAZING INSECTS

The scientists in the Entomology Department at the Smithsonian Institution study all kinds of insects. Here are some of the most intriguing.

MOST BEAUTIFUL: The sunset moth of Madagascar has a rainbow of colors and is widely admired for its beauty.

FASTEST FLYING: Dragonflies can travel 35 miles an hour. Hawk moths come in second at 33.7 miles an hour.

SMALLEST: A fairyfly wasp adult can be as tiny as .0067 of an inch long.

HEAVIEST: A goliath beetle from Africa weighs about three and a half ounces.

LONGEST: A giant stick insect's body measures thirteen inches, and when it stretches its legs it can reach up to twenty inches long.

LONGEST JUMPING: One species of flea can jump 150 times its body length.

LOUDEST: Some male cicadas can be heard for a quarter of a mile.

LONGEST LIVING: The queen termite lives for about fifty years. (Some scientists believe queens can live for as long as one hundred years!) Termite mounds also set records. One in Australia measured twenty feet high and one-hundred feet in diameter at the base.

LARGEST GROUP: Some 350,000 species of beetles have been identified.

Opposite: **Large elm leaf beetle.** Below: **Cicada.** Right: Termites in Australia can build enormous mounds with sand and saliva. The outside of the mound is rock-hard, while the nest inside stays cool and moist.

# BUZZ WORDS

ABDOMEN. The rear segment of an insect's body, which contains the organs for breathing, excreting wastes, and reproducing.

ANTENNAE. Sense organs on an insect's head used to smell, taste, feel, and hear.

ARACHNIDS. Animals such as spiders that have eight legs and a body divided into two segments. (An insect's body is divided into three segments, therefore spiders are not insects.)

ATTINI ANTS. A group of ants that plant and tend fungus gardens for food.

BENEFICIAL BUGS. Insects that feed or lay their eggs on insects that people consider harmful. When the eggs hatch, the offspring eat away at the bug they are living on and eventually kill it.

BLOW FLY. A common fly that deposits its eggs on dead bodies (carcasses).

CAMOUFLAGE. An adaptation some insects use to blend in with their environment and consequently protect themselves from predators.

CATERPILLAR. The wormlike larva of a butterfly or moth.

COMPOUND EYES. Insect eyes made up of many light-sensitive units, which provide a mosaic-like view of the world.

ENTOMOLOGY. The study of insects.

ENTOMOLOGIST. A scientist who studies insects.

EXOSKELETON. The outer hard shell that supports an insect's body.

FORENSIC ENTOMOLOGIST. A scientist who uses the predictable patterns of bug behavior and development to help solve crimes.

INSECT. An animal with an exoskeleton whose body is divided into three segments (head, thorax, and abdomen) and which has six legs, one or two pairs of wings, and two antennae.

LARVA. The early stage in the life cycle of insects such as flies during which they feed and grow.

MAGGOT. A fly larva.

MIMICRY. An adaptation used by some insects to copy or mimic the look of a more dangerous animal so that they can protect themselves from predators.

MYRMECOLOGIST. A scientist who studies ants.

POLLINATE. To fertilize with pollen.

PREDATOR. An animal that hunts and eats other animals.

PROBOSCIS. The hoselike mouthpart that some insects, such as butterflies and moths, use for feeding and sucking

PUPA. The cocoon stage in the life cycle of insects such as flies during which they transform into an adult.

SYMBIOSIS. The mutually beneficial relationship between two unlike organisms.

THORAX. An insect's middle segment, which carries its legs and wings.

TRACHEAE. The breathing tubes that carry oxygen throughout an insect's body.

GONE BUGGY?

Zebra caterpillar

To learn more about insects, check out these resources:

BOOKS

Bug Faces, by Darlyne A. Murawski (National Geographic Society, 2000).

An Extraordinary Life: The Story of a Monarch Butterfly, by Laurence Pringle (Orchard Books, 1997).

What's That Bug? by Nan Froman, illustrated by Julian Mulock (Little, Brown and Company, 2001).

Bugs in 3-D, by Mark Blum (Chronicle Books, 1998).

Pet Bugs: A Kid's Guide to Catching and Keeping Touchable Insects, by Sally Stenhouse Kneidel, illustrated by Mauro Magellan (John Wiley & Sons, 1994).

Caterpillars, Bugs and Butterflies (Take-Along Guide), by Mel Boring, illustrated by Linda Garrow (North Wood Press, 1999).

WEB SITES

Monarch Watch: www.MonarchWatch.org

Bugbios: www.bugbios.com

Insecta Inspecta World: www.insecta-inspecta.com

A virtual tour of the O. Orkin Insect Zoo at the Smithsonian Institution's National Museum of Natural History: www.mnh.si.edu/museum/VirtualTour/Tour/Second/InsectZoo

YOUNG ENTOMOLOGISTS SOCIETY

To meet other kids who are interested in insects and receive bulletins with the latest news about bugs, check out the Young Entomologists Society:

Web site: http://members.aol.com/YESbugs/bugclub.html
Address: 6907 West Grand River Ave.
Lansing, MI 48906-9131
Phone/Fax: 517-886-0630
e-mail: YESbugs@aol.com

INDEX